CONNECT

PATRIOTS AND REDCOATS

STORIES OF AMERICAN REVOLUTIONARY WAR LEADERS

BY STEVEN OTFINOSKI

Consultant:
Nathaniel Sheidley, PhD
Historian and Director of Public History
Bostonian Society
Boston, Massachusetts

CAPSTONE PRESS
a capstone imprint

Connect is published by Capstone Press,
1710 Roe Crest Drive, North Mankato, Minnesota 56003
www.capstonepub.com

Library of Congress Cataloging-in-Publication Data
Otfinoski, Steven.
Patriots and redcoats : stories of American revolutionary war leaders /
by Steven Otfinoski.
pages cm. — (Connect. The revolutionary war)
Summary: "Using the biography text structure, explores the key leaders of the
Revolutionary War"— Provided by publisher.
Includes bibliographical references and index.
ISBN 978–1–4914–2005–8 (library binding) — ISBN 978–1–4914–2158–1 (pbk.) —
ISBN 978–1–4914–2164–2 (ebook pdf)
1. United States—Politics and government—1775–1783—Juvenile literature. 2. United
States—History—Revolution, 1775–1783—Juvenile literature. 3. United States—
History—Revolution, 1775–1783—Biography—Juvenile literature. 4. Statesmen—
United States—Biography—Juvenile literature. 5. Generals—United States—
Biography—Juvenile literature. 6. Statesmen—Great Britain—Biography—Juvenile
literature. 7. Generals—Great Britain—Biography—Juvenile literature. 8. United
States—History—Revolution, 1775–1783—British forces—Juvenile literature. 9. United
States—History—Revolution, 1775–1783—Participation, Female—Juvenile literature.
I. Title.
E210.O84 2015
973.3092'2—dc23   2014026903

Editorial Credits
Jennifer Besel, editor; Veronica Scott, designer; Wanda Winch, media researcher;
    Charmaine Whitman, production specialist

Photo Credits
Archiving Early America, www.earlyamerica.com, 29 (right); Bridgeman Images:
Peter Newark American Pictures/Private Collection/Emanuel Gottlieb Leutze, cover;
Courtesy of Army Art Collection, U.S. Army Center of Military History, 27; Courtesy
of the Massachusetts Historical Society, 11 (bottom); CriaImages.com/Jay Robert
Nash Collection, 38 (left), 41; David R. Wagner, 44–45; Library of Congress: Prints and
Photographs Division, 6–7, 9, 11 (top), 12, 13, 14, 17, 23, 34, 35, 37, 39, Rare Books and
Special Collections Division, 31, 32, Thomas Jefferson Library, Rare Books and Special
Collections Division, 38 (r); National Archives and Records Administration, 29 (l),
ourdocuments.gov, 45; Newscom: akg–images, 10, 26, Prisma, 16; North Wind Picture
Archives, 43; Pamela Patrick White, www.ppatrickwhite.com, 15; Shutterstock:
Ekaterina Romanova, ornate frames, Ensuper, cover (background), Extezy (vintage
calligraphic elements), f–f–f–f (old calligraphic décor elements), GarryKillan (damask
ornamental designs), wacomka, vintage floral background); SuperStock: Crabbs
Historical Dictionary, 19; Thinkstock: iStockphoto/Steven Wynn, 25, Photos.com, 21,
33; www.historicalimagebank.com, Painting by Don Troiani, 4–5

Printed in the United States of America in Stevens Point, Wisconsin.
092014   008479WZS15

TABLE OF CONTENTS

A REVOLUTION BEGINS

"I wish to have no Connection with any Ship that does not Sail fast for I intend to go in harm's way."

—*from a letter written by navy leader John Paul Jones November 16, 1778*

The American Revolutionary War (1775–1783) was a bloody, eight-year battle for freedom. American colonists demanded representation in the British government that ruled them. When King George III refused, they demanded independence.

On the other side, Great Britain demanded loyalty from the colonists it had protected. The British government also felt colonists should help pay for that protection.

Eventually violence between American rebels, called Patriots, and British soldiers, nicknamed Redcoats, began to erupt throughout the colonies. In 1773 Patriots in Boston threw British tea into Boston Harbor to protest a tea tax. They destroyed more than 90,000 pounds (45 tons) of tea. Today that much tea would cost almost $1 million.

The British government struck back. **Parliament** closed Boston Harbor and sent more troops into the city. Colonists feared the soldiers and began stockpiling weapons.

By April 1775 tensions reached the breaking point. When British soldiers tried to seize weapons in Lexington, Massachusetts, colonists fought back. The American Revolution had begun.

Parliament—a group of people who make laws and run the government in some countries

Strong leaders—in politics and on the battlefield—arose on both sides. British and American leaders fought hard for their causes.

The goals and plan for U.S. independence were laid down by political leaders such as John Adams and Thomas Jefferson. Writers, such as Thomas Paine, used words to inspire colonists to fight. General George Washington led the fight on the battlefield, turning untrained colonists into toughened soldiers.

Colonists confronted British soldiers, in their recognizable red coats, many times during the American Revolutionary War.

The British, led by the forceful King George III, carried out a military campaign on American soil. Guided by experienced generals, such as William Howe and Henry Clinton, the British were a dominant force.

For eight years leaders from America and Great Britain battled with both words and weapons. Together they changed the course of history for two nations.

LEADERS IN POLITICS

Political leaders supported the battle with words, writings, and political action. These actions fueled the Revolution.

AMERICAN POLITICAL LEADERS

John Adams

Massachusetts lawyer John Adams became one of the most influential political leaders of the Revolution. He was known as a fair and courageous leader. But he was also very stubborn.

Before the war Adams spoke and wrote against British taxes on goods. But Great Britain continued to tax colonists without allowing them to have representatives in the government. So in 1774 the people of Massachusetts elected Adams to represent them at the first Continental Congress. The Congress was called to discuss what action to take against the British. At first Adams wanted to compromise with Great Britain. But he quickly became convinced independence was the only solution. He worked hard to convince his fellow **delegates** to break with Britain.

John Adams

delegate—someone who represents other people at a meeting

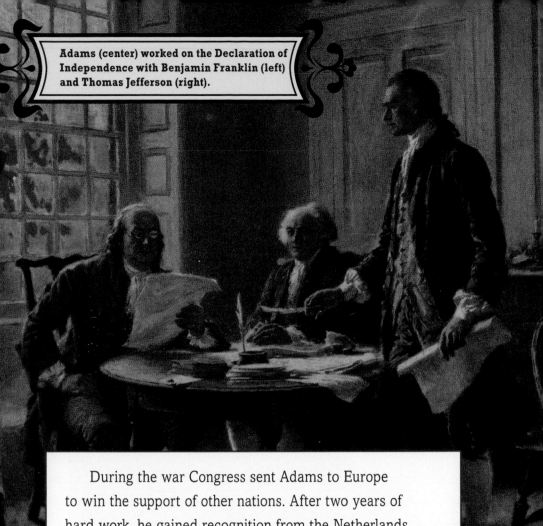
Adams (center) worked on the Declaration of Independence with Benjamin Franklin (left) and Thomas Jefferson (right).

During the war Congress sent Adams to Europe to win the support of other nations. After two years of hard work, he gained recognition from the Netherlands. Adams returned home with a loan of $2 million from the Netherlands to help the colonies finance the war.

But Adams' greatest achievements were in the area of law. Congress appointed him to the committee that wrote the Declaration of Independence. This document declared the colonies free from British rule.

During the war Adams served on nearly 90 committees, helping to shape the colonies' new government. After the war he continued to serve the nation he loved as its first vice president and second president. Many of his ideas still guide the United States today.

Leading for Women

While he was working toward colonial freedom, Adams' wife, Abigail, cared for their family and farm. During their long time apart, they wrote as many as 1,100 letters to each other.

In the letters Abigail proved to be a strong voice for women. She urged her husband to create a place for women in the new nation. She wrote to her husband in one letter, "... Remember the Ladies, and be more generous and favourable to them than your ancestors ... If perticuliar care and attention is not paid to the Laidies we ... will not hold ourselves bound by any Laws in which we have no voice, or Representation."

a letter from Abigail to her husband, dated March 31, 1776

11

Benjamin Franklin

A scientist, inventor, and author, Benjamin Franklin was one of the most celebrated Americans when the war began. He served for several years as an American representative in Britain, trying to bring peace. But when his efforts failed, he was as devoted to the cause of independence as his friend John Adams.

During the war Franklin went to France to gain an **alliance**. The French loved the witty, well-spoken Franklin, and he eventually convinced them to send troops to the colonies to fight for the American cause. This support was a huge help to the colonial war effort. With French help the colonists were able to defeat the well-trained British army.

Franklin's advice was sought by many, including the army's commander in chief George Washington. Franklin was a key leader in the development of the new United States. He helped write the Declaration of Independence and later the U.S. Constitution, among many other accomplishments. Today he is still remembered as a man with a good sense of humor and an unfailing commitment to his country.

Benjamin Franklin

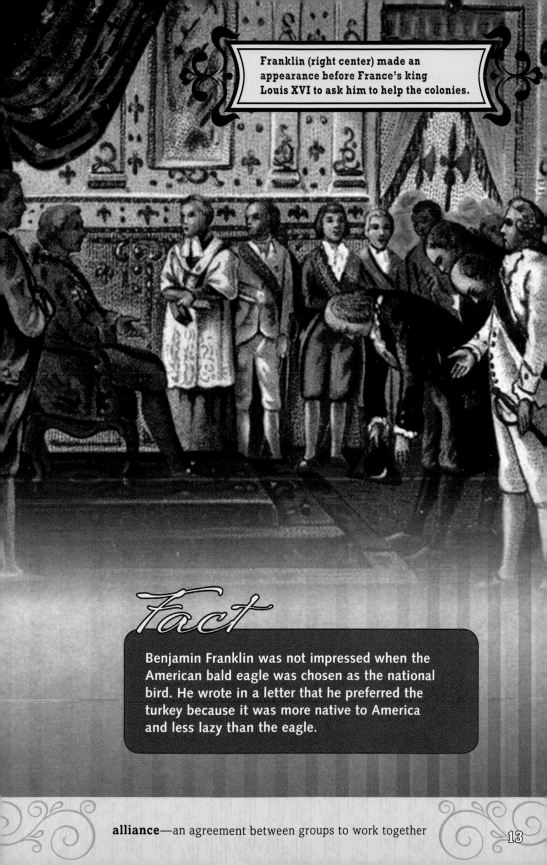

Franklin (right center) made an appearance before France's king Louis XVI to ask him to help the colonies.

Fact

Benjamin Franklin was not impressed when the American bald eagle was chosen as the national bird. He wrote in a letter that he preferred the turkey because it was more native to America and less lazy than the eagle.

alliance—an agreement between groups to work together

Thomas Jefferson

Thomas Jefferson was the great writer of the Revolution. In 1774 he wrote "A Summary View of the Rights of British America." In it, Jefferson argued that the colonies were not required to remain under the power of England's king and Parliament. Through that article Jefferson's talent for writing became clear.

Two years later Jefferson was chosen by the second Continental Congress to author the Declaration of Independence. Jefferson's elegant words officially declared Americans were within their rights to stand up for their liberty.

After the Congress ended, Jefferson returned to Virginia. During the war he was a leader in the state legislature and a strong spokesperson for a **republican** government. From 1779 to 1781, he served as Virginia's governor.

Thomas
Jefferson

republic—a political system in which officials are elected to represent citizens in government

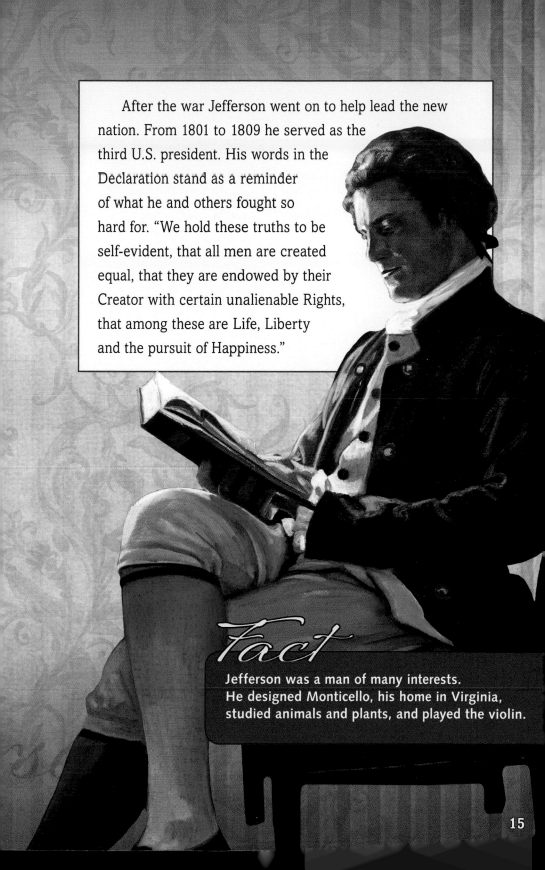

After the war Jefferson went on to help lead the new nation. From 1801 to 1809 he served as the third U.S. president. His words in the Declaration stand as a reminder of what he and others fought so hard for. "We hold these truths to be self-evident, that all men are created equal, that they are endowed by their Creator with certain unalienable Rights, that among these are Life, Liberty and the pursuit of Happiness."

Fact

Jefferson was a man of many interests. He designed Monticello, his home in Virginia, studied animals and plants, and played the violin.

King George III took the throne three years before the end of the French and Indian War (1754–1763). This war between Great Britain and France was fought in the American colonies. Both sides wanted control of North America. Eventually the British won over the French and their American Indian allies. But it was a costly war, and Britain was deeply in debt.

George needed to find ways to raise money to pay those debts. Through the 1760s and 1770s, he pressed his prime ministers to create new taxes for the colonies. But his rule was inconsistent. When colonists grew angry over the taxes, George ended them, only to create new ones. He also gave favors to leaders in Parliament who did what he wanted. This corruption angered colonists further.

When the Revolutionary War erupted, the king sent in troops and refused to compromise with colonists. He also kept the war going even after it was clear his army could not win.

Some historians believe George's inconsistencies may have been due to an illness. The king suffered from a disease that caused him to go temporarily insane. On top of this, George had a learning disability. He was a hard worker and fought to overcome the obstacles. But the stress of wars proved to be too much for him. He eventually went permanently insane.

King George III

Lord North

Lord North served as prime minister of Great Britain during the Revolutionary War. As prime minister North ran the everyday affairs of government. With his booming voice and quick humor, he was a close friend of King George.

In 1773 the British East India Tea Company was in danger of failing. North decided to rescue the company by sending its extra tea to the colonies. There the tea would be sold with a smaller tax than was on other teas. Colonists saw this as a move to control the tea they purchased. On December 16 Patriots dumped tea into Boston Harbor to protest North's move.

North was furious about the event that became known as the Boston Tea Party. He wrote new laws, called the Coercive Acts, to punish the colonists. He closed the harbor and brought in more troops. He also put a British supporter in office as Massachusetts' governor. The Coercive Acts angered people throughout the colonies.

Fact

Colonists called the Coercive Acts by a different name. They called them the "Intolerable Acts" because they felt they were intolerable, or impossible, to live with.

Lord North

Soon North realized that Great Britain was on the edge of war with its colonies. In January 1775 he offered a compromise. But it was too late. In April the first shots of war were fired. North grew more and more unhappy as the war dragged on. He tried to resign as prime minister several times. King George finally accepted North's resignation in 1782 after the British army met its major defeat in America at Yorktown.

Edmund Burke

As a member of Parliament, Edmund Burke spoke boldly for the rights of American colonists. In his powerful—but very long—speeches, Burke spoke in favor of working with colonists. He opposed taxes on them and said they should have all the rights of British subjects.

When war broke out, Burke opposed the use of force against the colonists. He correctly saw that the war would be disastrous for Great Britain. But North and other political leaders failed to listen.

Fact

Burke was a smart political leader, but he was not the best public speaker. His delivery was often awkward. And some of his speeches lasted more than eight hours.

Edmund Burke

MILITARY LEADERS

When the war began, British troops were trained, experienced soldiers. But they didn't know the land. America's soldiers were farmers and shopkeepers who barely knew how to fight. Leaders on both sides rose to the challenges and fought for their causes.

AMERICAN MILITARY LEADERS

George Washington took over the newly-formed Continental army in 1775. Through strong discipline and perseverance, he turned a group of untrained men into a proud and effective army.

But Washington was not a great military **tactician**. He lost as many battles as he won. One of his most disastrous defeats was at the Battle of Long Island in New York. To save his army from destruction, Washington made a swift retreat through New Jersey and Pennsylvania. It was then that he showed his strengths. On Christmas night 1776, Washington crossed the icy Delaware River. With 2,400 men he surprised the **Hessian** soldiers at Trenton, New Jersey. Confident and prepared, he beat the British a few days later at the Battle of Princeton.

Washington (standing) and his men broke up the ice on the Delaware River in order to cross and surprise the enemy.

For the rest of the war, Washington led his forces through bloody battles and horrible winters. After eight years of wins and losses, he brought his troops to a final victory over the British at Yorktown, Virginia.

After the war Washington's reputation as a hero and great leader followed him. The new nation chose him as its first president.

tactician—someone who makes a plan for fighting a battle
Hessian—a German soldier hired by the British

23

Letters from the Field

Washington and other leaders communicated through letters. Many of those letters survive today. They give a great look at what the people were going through. The following letter from Nathanael Greene to Washington shows the difficulty commanders had paying their soldiers.

Morris Town 3rd May 1780

Sir

Being again Destitute of Money, and the Expresses (who are in the same situation) having a considerable sum due to them, I am under the necessity of asking for another Warrant on the Military Chest for fifteen or twenty thousand Dollars: if this can be granted, the public service will be benefited, and I much obliged. With great Respect, I am Your Excellency's Most Obedient & Humble Servent

Nath. Greene

Q.M.G.

Nathanael Greene

Washington's most trusted commander was Nathanael Greene. Greene grew up as a member of the peace-loving Quaker religion in Rhode Island. But in 1774, with the possibility of war looming, Greene organized a **militia**. He was expelled from the Quakers for his actions.

Greene proved himself a tough fighter. He fought bravely at the battles of Trenton in New Jersey and Brandywine and Germantown in Pennsylvania. He also proved to be very good at getting military supplies. In 1778 Greene was promoted to Quartermaster General of the Continental army. In that role he was given the task of getting supplies to troops across the colonies.

In 1780 Washington sent Greene to North Carolina to reorganize the Southern forces. With brilliant leadership Greene used the state militia to drive British General Charles Cornwallis out of the state. Cornwallis marched into Virginia where he met his final defeat at Yorktown. Greene's reputation after the war was nearly as good as Washington's.

Nathanael Greene

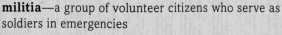

John Paul Jones

The Revolution produced no greater naval leader than John Paul Jones. Born in Scotland, Jones came to America in 1773 and joined the small Continental navy. A fierce fighter, Jones captured eight British ships and sank eight others in one six-week period in 1776.

On September 23, 1779, Jones encountered a British warship off England's coast. He knew the warship had cannons he could not beat. So Jones ordered his ship to ram into the British ship. The British captain asked Jones if he was surrendering. "Sir," Jones replied, "I have not yet begun to fight." Jones and his crew took over the British ship and abandoned their damaged ship, which quickly sank.

John Paul Jones

Fact

A big hero, John Paul Jones is believed to have been no taller than 5 foot, 5 inches (165 centimeters). Thomas Jefferson called him "Little Jones."

"Mad" Anthony Wayne

General Anthony Wayne was given the nickname "Mad" from the men he led. He was known for his fierce determination and fiery personality.

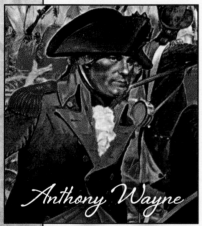

Anthony Wayne

Wayne was a wealthy businessman before he joined the colonists' fight for freedom. In 1775 he brought a **regiment** of soldiers to Canada to fight the British. He was made a colonel in the Continental army in 1776 for his fighting spirit.

On July 16, 1779, Wayne led his weary men through a swamp at night. They surprised British troops at Stony Point, New York. In the end the Americans took the fort and captured more than 400 British soldiers. The victory was just the boost colonists needed.

Wayne helped defeat the British at the Battle of Yorktown in Virginia. Later he also beat the British and their American Indian allies in Georgia. Wayne's legacy lives on in at least seven American cities named after him, including Fort Wayne, Indiana.

regiment—a large group of soldiers who fight together as a unit

27

Benedict Arnold

Benedict Arnold could have been one of the great American heroes of the Revolution. Instead, he ended up its worst **traitor**. Arnold was a courageous soldier who led his men bravely in an attack on Canada and at the battle of Ridgefield, Connecticut. Arnold felt his actions deserved to be rewarded. But Washington and others passed him up for promotions.

Eventually Arnold was put in command of a fort in Philadelphia. There he became friends with Loyalists faithful to the British. He also made some bad business deals to try to become wealthy.

Arnold was **court-martialed** for his dishonest business deals, but he was allowed to return to command. Arnold was angry by how he had been treated. The general turned traitor.

Arnold planned to turn over West Point, an American military fort in New York, to the British. But his plot was found out before he could act. Arnold fled to a British warship. He led raids against Americans before sailing to England in December 1781. He never returned to America.

Benedict Arnold

Poſtſcript.

As the famous Gen. ARNOLD has abandoned the REBEL Service, and joined our Army at NEW YORK, we preſent our Readers with his Addreſs to the Inhabitants of America, taken from RIVINGTON'S ROYAL NEW YORK GAZETTE, of Oct. 21, 1780.

To the INHABITANTS of AMERICA.

I SHOULD forfeit, even in my own opinion, the place I have ſo long held in yours, if I could be indifferent to your approbation, and ſilent on the motives which have induced me to join the King's arms.

A very few words, however, ſhall ſuffice upon a ſubject ſo perſonal; for to the thouſands who ſuffer under the tyranny of the uſurpers in the revolted provinces, as well as to the great multitude who have long wiſhed for its ſubverſion, this inſtance of my conduct can want no vindication; and as to the claſs of men who are criminally protracting the war from ſiniſter views at the expence of the public intereſt, I prefer their enmity to their applauſe. I am, therefore, only concerned in this addreſs, to explain myſelf t; ſuch of my countrymen, as want abilities, or opportunities, to detect the artifices by which they are duped.

Having fought by your ſide when the love of our country animated our arms; I ſhall expect, from your juſtice and candour, what your deceivers, with more art and leſs honeſty, will find it inconſiſtent with their own views to admit.

When I quitted domeſtic happineſs for the perils of the field, I conceived the rights of my country in danger, and that duty and honour called me to her defence. A redreſs of grievances was my only object and aim; however, I acquieſced in a ſtep which I thought precipitate, the declaration of independence: to juſtify this meaſure, many plauſible reaſons were urged, which could no longer exiſt, when Great Britain, with the open arms of a parent, offered to embrace us as children, and grant the wiſhed-for redreſs.

Arnold wrote a letter to the people in America, defending his actions. The letter was printed in a New York newspaper in October 1780 and in a London newspaper in November.

traitor—someone who aids the enemy of his of her country
court-martial—when a military member goes to court for committing a crime

29

BRITISH MILITARY LEADERS

William Howe

British General William Howe became a well-known military leader during the American Revolution. But before he fought against the colonists, he actually supported them in Parliament.

Howe was a representative in Parliament. When prime minister North introduced the Coercive Acts, Howe spoke against them. He said that Great Britain should make peace with the colonies.

However Howe was also a strong military leader. He had fought in the French and Indian War and other conflicts. His commanding officers sent him to the colonies in 1775 despite his feelings.

In America Howe drove Washington out of New York in the Battle of Long Island. He went on to defeat Washington again at the battles of Brandywine and Germantown in Pennsylvania.

But Howe failed to fully defeat Washington's forces. The government began criticizing his actions. He resigned from his command in 1778 and returned to England.

William
Howe

Sir Henry Clinton

Henry Clinton took command of British forces when Howe left. Clinton was incredibly shy and found it hard to clearly share his ideas. But he was a smart tactician. Clinton realized he couldn't defeat the French fleet that had come to help the colonists. So he focused his efforts on the South. In December 1779 he attacked Charleston, South Carolina, taking the city and capturing 5,400 American soldiers. It was his greatest achievement in the war, but it wasn't enough to win.

Clinton was blamed at the war's end for losing the colonies in the battle of Yorktown. However, it was Clinton's second-in-command, General Charles Cornwallis, who was actually responsible for that defeat. After returning to England, Clinton wrote his own version of events to regain his reputation. He succeeded and was made a full general in 1793.

Sir Henry Clinton

Charles Cornwallis

An ambitious military leader, Charles Cornwallis served successfully under General Howe. When Howe stepped down, Cornwallis expected to take over. Instead, Clinton got the job. Cornwallis and Clinton did not get along.

Cornwallis had helped capture New York in 1776. He later went on to defeat General Horatio Gates' army at Camden, South Carolina. Confident in his abilities, Cornwallis disobeyed Clinton's orders and marched into Virginia in 1781.

Charles Cornwallis

In Yorktown, Virginia, Cornwallis and his men were trapped by American and French forces. He expected to be supported by the British fleet by sea, but it never arrived. Cornwallis surrendered on October 19, 1781, in the last major battle of the war. The British government later cleared him of blame for losing the battle.

Defending Their Land

Joseph Brant, also known as Thayendanegea, was an American Indian leader who fought with the British during the Revolutionary War. As a teen Brant joined the British Army and fought in the French and Indian War. He proved to be a powerful leader and earned the title of Mohawk chief.

As war between colonists and British soldiers began, Brant and other American Indian leaders had to decide what side to take. Brant wanted to defend the Iroquois land above all else. So he relied on the relationships he had built with the British. Leading four Iroquois tribes, Brant and his warriors fought bravely for the British. But when the British lost the war, so did the American Indians. When the Treaty of Paris was signed, ending the Revolutionary War, the British lost their claim over the Iroquois lands. The land went to the new United States. All the promises Great Britain had made to Brant were broken.

Joseph Brant

John Burgoyne

John Burgoyne was nicknamed "Gentleman Johnny" by his men for his good manners and gentle treatment of his men. Burgoyne came up with a plan to split the colonies in half and win the war. In June 1777 he came down from Canada with up to 10,000 soldiers to take Albany, New York. General Clinton and his army were to meet up with him there. But Clinton didn't arrive in time. Burgoyne quickly found himself surrounded by American troops. He was forced to surrender on October 17 at Saratoga, New York. Gentleman Johnny was taken prisoner of war. This defeat was a major loss for the British.

Created around 1852, this print re-creates the scene where General Burgoyne surrendered his sword after the Battles of Saratoga.

CITIZEN LEADERS

Local leaders played an important part in the war too. Some formed small bands of fighters. Others fought the enemy with words or by keeping homes running.

Before the war started, Ethan Allen was at war with other colonists. He staked a claim for Vermont and wanted to make it a separate colony. But New York also claimed Vermont as its own. Allen formed the Green Mountain Boys, a group of local fighting men, to drive out New Yorkers who settled on Vermont land. When war broke out, Allen joined the Patriot cause.

Early on the morning of May 10, 1775, Allen and Colonel Benedict Arnold led an attack on the British Fort Ticonderoga. The British were half asleep and put up little resistance. A British officer demanded to know who approved the invasion of the fort. Allen replied, "In the name of the Great Jehovah [God] and the Continental Congress!" It was one of the first American successes in the war.

Allen (standing over table) with his Green Mountain Boys

Writing for Patriots

Mercy Otis Warren was a powerful voice for the Patriot cause. She wrote plays, poems, and essays supporting the war effort. She also wrote speeches for her husband, James Warren, who was speaker of the Massachusetts House of Representatives.

In 1788 Warren wrote a pamphlet outlining what she disliked about the new nation's Constitution. Many believe that her book helped push lawmakers to create the Bill of Rights that guarantees certain freedoms to all people.

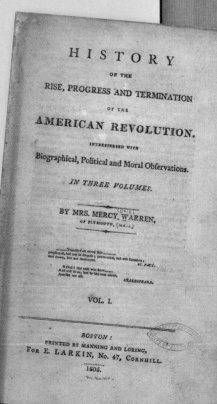

HISTORY

OF THE

RISE, PROGRESS AND TERMINATION

OF THE

AMERICAN REVOLUTION.

INTERSPERSED WITH

Biographical, Political and Moral Observations.

IN THREE VOLUMES.

BY MRS. MERCY WARREN,

OF PLYMOUTH, (MASS.)

ST. PAUL.

SHAKESPEARE.

VOL. I.

BOSTON:

PRINTED BY MANNING AND LORING,

FOR E. LARKIN, No. 47, CORNHILL.

1805.

Warren's *History of the Rise, Progress and Termination of the American Revolution* gave a thorough look at the war from causes to effects. Historians still use this work to understand the viewpoint of someone who lived through the events.

Thomas Paine

Thomas Paine, an Englishman, came to the colonies in 1774 to work as a magazine editor. In 1776, months before the Declaration of Independence was written, Paine wrote a pamphlet called *Common Sense*. In his work Paine argued for American independence. He wrote that not only was independence good for America, but it would serve as a shining example for the entire world. Paine's work influenced many colonists to fight for independence.

Paine continued to write works that inspired American Patriots. He later served as secretary to the foreign affairs committee of the Continental Congress. But Paine was a difficult man to get along with. He spent time after the Revolution in England and France. When he finally returned to the United States, he quarreled with nearly everyone, including President George Washington.

Thomas Paine

George Rogers Clark

George Rogers Clark's victories on the battlefield helped win the war. They also won a whole area of land that would expand the new nation.

In 1778 Clark was a frontiersman living in what is now Kentucky. He led a small band of men into British-held territory northwest of the Ohio River. Clark seized two British outposts in present-day Illinois. Then he marched on the British fort at Vincennes in what is now Indiana. The British were completely taken by surprise and surrendered. It was a stunning victory that lifted American spirits.

Clark went on to more victories. He saved St. Louis from the British. Then in present-day Ohio, he drove back the Shawnee Indians who were British allies. Clark's efforts opened present-day Ohio, Illinois, Indiana, Michigan, Wisconsin, and parts of Minnesota to American settlement.

Fact

Clark's younger brother was William Clark, coleader of the famed Lewis and Clark Expedition (1804–1806).

British general James Inglis Hamilton (right) surrendered to Clark (left) after the battle at Vincennes.

Francis Marion

Things looked dark for Americans when the British took over Charleston, South Carolina, in 1780. But they had a champion who wouldn't give up.

Francis Marion was a captain in a South Carolina regiment. After helping to defend Fort Sullivan in Charleston Harbor, he stayed to command the fort for three years. In March 1780 Marion was at a dinner party in Charleston when he fell and broke his ankle. It was a lucky accident. Marion left Charleston to heal in the country. He was gone when the British took over Charleston that May.

Marion and his men fled into the northern part of the state. They were too small a force to battle the British head on, so they used **guerrilla** tactics. Marion would conduct quick raids on the British and then disappear into the Carolina swamps. Lieutenant Colonel Banastre Tarleton tried time and again to capture Marion. The frustrated British commander gave the crafty Marion the nickname "Swamp Fox."

guerrilla—warfare using small, surprise attacks rather than large battles

Marion, also known as the "Swamp Fox," led his soldiers through the rough land to surprise enemy forces.

Fact

Francis Marion's soldiers had little money for weapons and ammunition. Their swords were made from saw blades and their bullets from melted pewter plates.

WAR ENDS, A NATION BEGINS

The Battle of Yorktown did not entirely end the American Revolution. Fighting dragged on in a number of places, but by the spring of 1782 negotiations for peace were underway. Patriot leaders during the war became leaders of the new United States of America. British leaders accepted their defeat at the hands of the American colonies.

Leaders of the American Revolution are remembered as heroes for standing up for their beliefs. It was a long and deadly conflict. But today Britain and America are strong allies, proud of the common heritage they share.

Leaders signed the Treaty of Paris in 1783. The treaty declared the colonies were free from British rule.

1783 Treaty of Paris

Glossary

alliance (uh-LY-uhnts)—an agreement between groups to work together

court-martial (KORT-MAR-shuhl)—when a military member goes to court for committing a crime

delegate (DEL-uh-guht)—someone who represents other people at a meeting

guerrilla (guh-RIL-ah)—warfare using small, surprise attacks rather than large battles

Hessian (HE-shun)—a German soldier hired by the British

militia (muh-LISH-uh)—a group of volunteer citizens who serve as soldiers in emergencies

Parliament (PAR-luh-muhnt)—a group of people who make laws and run the government in some countries

regiment (REJ-uh-muhnt)—a large group of soldiers who fight together as a unit

republic (ri-PUHB-lik)—a political system in which officials are elected to represent citizens in government

tactician (tac-TI-shun)—someone who makes a plan for fighting a battle

traitor (TRAY-tur)—someone who aids the enemy of his or her country

Internet Sites

FactHound offers a safe, fun way to find Internet sites related to this book. All of the sites on FactHound have been researched by our staff.

Here's all you do:

Visit *www.facthound.com*

Type in this code: 9781491420058

48

READ MORE

Gunderson, Jessica. *A Rebel Among Redcoats: A Revolutionary War Novel*. The Revolutionary War. North Mankato, Minn.: Stone Arch Books, 2015.

Levin, Jack E. *George Washington: The Crossing*. New York: Threshold Editions, 2013.

Perritano, John. *The Causes of the American Revolution*. Understanding the American Revolution. New York: Crabtree Publishing Company, 2013.

CRITICAL THINKING USING THE COMMON CORE

1. How did King George III differ from Edmund Burke in his attitude toward the colonists? Use other sources to support your answer.
   (Integration of Knowledge and Ideas)

2. Why was George Washington a great military leader despite losing a number of important battles? Use specific events and incidents to support your answer.
   (Integration of Knowledge and Ideas)

3. What effect did George Rogers Clark's victories at Vicennes and St. Louis have on the future of the United States?
   (Key Ideas and Details)

INDEX

Primary sources appear on the following pages:

Pages 4, 26, from *John Paul Jones: A Sailor's Biography* by Samuel Eliot Morison. (Boston: Little, Brown and Company, 1959).

Page 11, from letter from Abigail Adams to John Adams. March 31, 1776. Online by the Massachusetts Historical Society. www.masshist.org/digitaladams/ archive/doc?id=L17760331aa&bc=%2Fdigitaladams%2Farchive%2Fbrowse%2Fl etters_1774_1777.php

Page 15, from the Declaration of Independence. July 4, 1776. Online by the National Archives. www.archives.gov/exhibits/charters/declaration.html

Page 24, from letter from Nathanael Greene to George Washington. May 3, 1780. Online by The University of Virginia Press. http://rotunda.upress.virginia.edu/ founders/default.xqy?keys=FOEA-print-01-01-02-1644

Page 37, from "Ethan Allen Captures Fort Ticonderoga, 1775," EyeWitness to History, www.eyewitnesstohistory.com (2010).